HEAR

KENDALL THOMPSON WITH POEMS BY VICTORIA THOMPSON

MW01171945

POEMS BY KENDALL THOMPSON and VICTORIA THOMPSON

POEMS BY KENDALL THOMPSON and VICTORIA THOMPSON

Table of Contents

POEMS BY KENDALL THOMPSON and VICTORIA THOMPSON

Foreword

We will all have to deal with the death of a loved one. We will have to come to terms with losing someone. We will have to also come to terms with our own death. It will arrive! Will we hear the whispers of our ancestors? Will we hear the whispers of those who have taken the journey, before us? Hearing Whispers is a part of our journey.

POEMS BY KENDALL THOMPSON and VICTORIA THOMPSON

We live our lives knowing that one day we will be gone, while our loved ones continue on!

For
Mom (Irene Drayton Thompson)
For
Dad (Clayton Thompson Sr.)
for
Jeffrey Thompson
and
Norma Cheryl Thompson Blackmon

Poems

I'll write them, if you'll read them

Let you interpret what you've read

The words, I put to paper, should bring thought into your head

I didn't miss a comma, there was no word left out

I purposely misspelled a word, to bring about, more thought

Mine rhyme, because I want them to, there is no master scheme

Some come to me while running, some come to me in dreams

I'll write them, if you'll read them

My explanation as to how they're formed

My thoughts just seem to come to me and they come to me in Poems

Written by Kendall Thompson
10-14-2018

Tomorrow's Sunrise

Let you enjoy the sunrise
The sunrise that has been last seen

There is so much time till next sunrise
So many things could change

There is no guarantee you'll make it
Your eyesight just might not exist

Tomorrow's sunrise not promised
So it remains on my bucket list

I want to see the sunrise
Tomorrow's will be just fine

Once tomorrow's has been seen by me
I would love to see tomorrow's sunrise

 POEMS BY KENDALL THOMPSON and VICTORIA THOMPSON

My Mind's Picture

I want to enjoy the sunrise,
as it chases away the rain

I like knowing that the blood is blue,
as it races through my veins

I need to take the stairs
as the elevator doors part

I like knowing that a human being
is a priceless work of art

My mind will take the picture,
my description, is how I will share

Might you see my thoughtfulness
by the expression that I wear

My feet are soothed by water,
that's warmed by the heat from the sun

My mind is eased by writing poems,
mind's thoughts
from whence they come

POEMS BY KENDALL THOMPSON and VICTORIA THOMPSON

Tears from Our Angels

Heavenly raindrops from the skies

I hope they're tears from the angels' eyes

A soaking rain for those with faith

Awash with hope and saving grace

Let each know the power of love

The raindrops are tears from the heavens above

Let the angels' tears soothe your pain

Tears from our angels, why would they cry for us?

They are in heavens gates; they've felt God's touch!

 POEMS BY KENDALL THOMPSON and VICTORIA THOMPSON

Sunrise

One incredible moment,
All things are blessed to share

Moving gracefully above the horizon
Bringing a glow and awesome glare

Waited on by millions
A pristine a lordly show

Preparing to provide the light of day
With its awe-inspiring glow

 POEMS BY KENDALL THOMPSON and VICTORIA THOMPSON

Rest Easy

You've done all that you were placed here to do
Perhaps you've done much, much more

You've carried us through some tough times
You've mothered more than just yours

You've welcomed every neighbor
Beneath your table, laid strangers' feet

When you loved, you loved us all
You ensured that we all did eat

Now it's your turn to rest easy
It's our turn to carry the load

We will follow every instruction
We will do just as we were told

Rest easy, let you not worry
We will cry but not for long

The life you lived exemplary
It is those examples that will help us carry on!

POEMS BY KENDALL THOMPSON and VICTORIA THOMPSON

Last Call

Arms are open to greet me
My journey is now complete

The call I ran became my last
but please don't worry for me

Worry for my family, my son, my daughter, my wife

I will receive a hero's welcome,
but my leaving has changed their lives

They won't see that I am with them
They may not know I am now always there

I have gained my wings to protect them
I need them never to fear

My brothers and sisters will support you
They will ensure that you make it to the prom

They will be there to support you, as I will
So know you will never be alone!

 POEMS BY KENDALL THOMPSON and VICTORIA THOMPSON

Heavenly Angel

An angel resides in heaven
There must be heaven on earth

Your aura and your presence felt, since your day of birth

When heaven comes to reclaim you
When it is said your time has come

You will just be headed home, for it is heaven where you are from

I've known your earthly presence
Your body, too frail to hold your soul

Spread your wings and take to flight
You have a new home to explore

An angel in the heavens, watching over me

The place where now, you'll run your miles, and your spirit will run free

My angel resides in heaven

There was a time, I was sure, there was heaven on earth

The time is now to spread your wings
Exalt in your rebirth!

 POEMS BY KENDALL THOMPSON and VICTORIA THOMPSON

The Grand Reunion

Awash in tears for you father

It is your time; you have been called home

Knowing your love in our lifetime

You're in our hearts so we are never alone

We will still shed tears for you leaving

It's because we don't want you to go

Selfishly wanting more time with you

It's your love that we will forever know!

We cry for you've gone on to glory

It was time for you to go join our mom

I envision a grand reunion

You two have been apart way too long!

POEMS BY KENDALL THOMPSON and VICTORIA THOMPSON

<u>Costly!</u>

My eyes are heavy with tear drops
My voice cracks for I am at a loss

Another hero has paid the price
Another has paid the mighty cost

His loved ones know how to miss him
There are no holidays

She may just miss a Christmas
This is part of the price that is paid

The final price lays most heavy
My heart can't hold this weight

The loss of life is a costly loss
It's a chance that we are willing to take

We hope to retire healthy
We hope to live a life that is long

Some of us will, most of us don't
Those who don't have paid a mighty cost!

POEMS BY KENDALL THOMPSON and VICTORIA THOMPSON

Etched Within

I know, that now, you're forever sleeping and for this reason I cannot sleep

My eyes are heavy with moisture, they overflow, and I constantly weep

I know you're forever with me, but I can't help to feel you've been taken away

I have the courage to carry on, but for the strength, I will have to pray

I know, in time, less painful, this hurt, that is in my heart

It's only the difference between life and death, the only things, that could keep us apart

For now, I will say see you later, there is so much more that I need to say

I will let the memories wash over me, you are forever etched within my memories!

Brotherly Love

We walked together in perilous places
We stood our ground when there was ground to be held

You lifted me up when I needed lifting
You held me close when I needed to be held

We threw rocks and we also made sling shots
The boomerangs, we made, never worked

We grew up in the streets of our neighborhood
We progressed to be men of our church

We traveled and enjoyed each other's company
I expected that we'd have more time

The maker reaps as he sees fit
In our eyes, there's no reason or rhyme

Your time to go home came before mine
The streetlights must have made you race home

I will tell you that, my brother, I'll miss you
You're in my heart but I will still feel alone!

POEMS BY KENDALL THOMPSON and VICTORIA THOMPSON

Vigilance

We sit vigilant by your bedside
We stand ready to heed the call

This is what you would do for us
We are family, after all

There sits a brother and sister
Over there sits a niece, cousin, and aunt

You're being fed by a sister-in-law
Well deserved, this vigilance

Your husband is at the ready
His patience has been tried but he is true

In the shadows an army awaits
A nephew, your mother-in-law too

We sit vigilant by your bedside
We will be ready to take a stance

This is what you would do for us
So, we are steadfastly vigilant!

POEMS BY KENDALL THOMPSON and VICTORIA THOMPSON

Slamming Death's Door

I thought death's door was open
You walked up to it and slammed it closed

You can't tell how long someone will live
This information is not for a mortal to know

One moment a dire prognosis, the next moment, the outlook has changed

One thing that is known for certain
You pray in Jesus's name

Death's door, I thought was open, you walked up and slammed it closed

You have made it, very obvious, that it isn't your time to go

When you ascend your heavenly stairway, it will be you, who is ready to climb

For now, put away that welcome mat
She is not ready and it is not her time!

POEMS BY KENDALL THOMPSON and VICTORIA THOMPSON

Amongst the Angels

Soar amongst the angels
This is your destiny

You're no longer chained to a body
Your soul has now been set free

The winds will help you soar
On those winds, wings take flight

Watching over your loved ones
We are forever in your sight

An angel as you lived
A guardian as you have been reborn

The time for us a difficult one
We must and will carry on

Soar amongst the angels
This is your rightful place

I hope your Sisters, Mother and Aunts
I hope all are there to open the gate!

 POEMS BY KENDALL THOMPSON and VICTORIA THOMPSON

Family Reunion

Stately in her presence
Poised as she spoke her truth

Stubborn almost to a fault
An educator through and through

A daughter to a doting mother
A sister to brothers, one gone

All leaving one brother, to live a life
Seemingly leaving him alone

Know that she didn't just leave you
She is gone to do the things she's done before

She will be there, to greet you, when you show up
She will be there to open the door

There you will find the whole family
Father, mother, brother and sister too

All will sit at the dinner table
They are saving a setting for you!

In Flight

I have earned my wings
I am finally ready to soar

No earthly bonds can hold me down
No pain, forever more

This day was on my schedule
My wings had been sized and stored

My bags are packed, I am ready
I have a new world to explore

The ringing of the bells
All saints this is our night

We soar throughout the heavens
I have my wings and I am in flight

POEMS BY KENDALL THOMPSON and VICTORIA THOMPSON

He is with You

Let his peace be with you
Let your heart be filled

That now he gets the rest deserved
Let his soul forever be still

Now he finished his journey
His destination, he has arrived

In your heart he will forever remain
In this way he will always survive

Let his peace be with you
Remember what in you, he instilled

Let you finish your journey
Every wish in your life be fulfilled!

POEMS BY KENDALL THOMPSON and VICTORIA THOMPSON

In your Heart

Smile because it's time
Time to let the anger go

Knowing that the loss of her
You would have no other know

The mirror that you look in,
Should always see her face

Her smile is your and your smile hers
The place you shared, her space

Know, she will never leave you
She will always be a part

Her arms will remain in an everlasting hug
Her heart beats in your heart

Know we know not, your sorrow
In life each sorrow owned

Know that we all feel your pain
For this reason, you will never be alone!

POEMS BY KENDALL THOMPSON and VICTORIA THOMPSON

It's My Turn

It's my turn to make the journey
It's my turn to lie in state

It's my turn to be mourned
It's my turn to come face to face

It's my turn to meet my maker
It's my turn to bask in the sun

It's my turn to no longer live in pain
It's my turn to travel home

It's my turn to sing God's praises
It's my turn to be set free

It's my turn to see our parents and the
others that have journeyed home before me

It's my turn to say see you later
It's my turn to close my eyes

It's my turn to say, " don't cry for me"
It's my turn, so please don't cry!

POEMS BY KENDALL THOMPSON and VICTORIA THOMPSON

Sized and Stored

You have protected man and country
You have stood up for friend and foe

Taught that blood is thicker than water
Family first is what we know

Mom and Dad has left a legacy
Sisters and brothers must carry it on

The fruits of their labor is ours to share
Never ours to hold a grudge upon

Brick and mortar makes memories
Time will crumble these things

Money, too, becomes less important, when we realize that we all will gain
our wings

Hold dear your friends and family
Blood is thicker than the mud

Make more memories before they're gone
Our wings have been sized and stored!

POEMS BY KENDALL THOMPSON and VICTORIA THOMPSON

<u>Come to me!</u>

Come home to me, my humble servant
You have completed your earthly deeds

Now is the time to rest your soul
It is now time to fulfill your needs

It is time to bask in God's glory
Into the sun and out of the shade

It's time to let yourself relax
Come home and don't be afraid

I can see your eyes are heavy
Let, from your eyes, your tears release

I can see your earthly pain
I can see your family weep

There is anger in your exchanges
This is one of the greatest unknowns

It's an individual journey and each
will have to make this journey alone

Come home my humble servant
Let yourself be free

You have completed your earthly deeds
It is time you come home to me!

 POEMS BY KENDALL THOMPSON and VICTORIA THOMPSON

Heavy Eyes

My eyes can't hold the weight of my tears
I hold them back, but my eyes still weep

I will cry, with you, if you want me too
I will shed tears, for you, if that is the need

I will stand guard beside you
I will back you till the end

I will carry you if that is the need
You will never have to walk again

I will feed you when you're hungry
I will be your punching bag

I will gently anger you, for I am also sad

My eyes are truly heavy, so for now I will just sit and cry

I will prepare when our moment arrives, and we say our earthly
goodbye!

POEMS BY KENDALL THOMPSON and VICTORIA THOMPSON

Puzzlingly

You will never see all of its pieces
There is a puzzle made, for each, that lives

The puzzle pieces have been misplaced
Over time each will find hers or his

Pieces are made of life's main moments
The pieces shaped, as one, lives life

It is puzzling how they perfectly fit
Some are made of happy times, others are shaped by sadness and strife

Life is a jigsaw puzzle
Life's moments create the pieces that fit

In the end all pieces will fit into place
In the end it is no longer puzzling!

POEMS BY KENDALL THOMPSON and VICTORIA THOMPSON

Nothing to Fear

I heard you, although, in a whisper
"I am ready to go home"

I am not with you, in your thoughts, but I need you to know, you're not
alone

You have your angels on your shoulders
You have family by your side

You have your courage, you have your faith
You still have the rest of your life

So, although, it was heard in a whisper
Your statement, heard loud and clear

"I am ready to journey home"
"I have nothing left to fear!

POEMS BY KENDALL THOMPSON and VICTORIA THOMPSON

Safely Home

I have made it safely into the house of God
I have made it safely home

I know that you've been worried
I had to make the journey all alone

When I arrived, the door was opened
You were worried I didn't have a key

I was greeted by our ancestors
The entire family tree

There sits our mother and our father
There sits our grandparents on both sides

Our aunts and uncles welcomed me
I couldn't remember all our cousins' names, but I tried

We shook hands and hugged each other
Our brother made some jokes

I wanted you to know I was safely home
No need to worry anymore!

POEMS BY KENDALL THOMPSON and VICTORIA THOMPSON

Weepingly Sleep

Tonight is like few others
Tonight I will weepingly sleep

I will sadly remember the moments
I will remember that the reaper must reap

My eyes will over flowingly well
I will be short of breath and unable to breathe

I will lay down, albeit, restlessly
Tonight, I will weepingly sleep

Somber Thoughts

I am sullen and full of gloom
My days are dark and full of despair

My thoughts are somber and dark
The starless sky and the deathly cold air

The reaper has come to reap
Is it our time to give our fair share

There is no blanket to cover this type of cold
Somber thoughts seemingly everywhere

POEMS BY KENDALL THOMPSON and VICTORIA THOMPSON

The Final Alarm

I am first due on this box alarm
Second due, pickup my line

I have trained for years to make this run
I need you to know I'll be fine

I have run a call a time or two
Just know, this one will be my last

I am reporting to the sector chief
I am handing him my P.A.S.S.

The next call that I am toned out for
I will respond from the heavens above

I will respond with wings of an angel
I will protect all those that I love

POEMS BY KENDALL THOMPSON and VICTORIA THOMPSON

Periods of Quiet

The quietness heightens my senses

I wait for movement to allay my fears

Have you gone on to glory, are you simply resting, your mind and ears?

There are periods of quiet

The lulls in sound, will test your faith

I can't tell when you are looking

Then a crooked smile shows on your face

Then a period of quiet

This lull in sound, for which I wait

Homeward bound your destination

It is not I who will determine the time or place

The periods of quiet, I look for movement to allay my fears

The periods of quiet, lets me know your time is near!

 POEMS BY KENDALL THOMPSON and VICTORIA THOMPSON

When You Can't

When you can't lift your hands, I will feed you

When you can't lift your feet, it is then, I will carry

When you can't lift your eyelids, I will describe what I see

Let all these be, the least of your worries

When you can't lift your voice, I will speak up for you, for I know, how you let your thoughts be known

When you can't lift the knocker, I will open up the door

I will walk with you, till you're fully inside, your new home!

POEMS BY KENDALL THOMPSON and VICTORIA THOMPSON

<u>Goodbye</u>

I have cried, over and over, inside my mind

Will there ever be a more appropriate time, to cry

Out loud, I make it known, you will leave us, but we will never be alone, I will see you again

In my dreams, of yesterday, I watched as a baby, waiting for my turn to also play, outside

There is sun, rain, sleet and snow, it is not us who will choose our time to go, home

It is where we long to be, no more pain and no more sorrow, for me

This is where I made my play, there was no longer a need for me to stay, Goodbye

I now will say my last farewell, my last hello, I wish you well!

Goodbye

POEMS BY KENDALL THOMPSON and VICTORIA THOMPSON

We Will Meet Again

I watch and I stare in amazement, as you fight the final fight

I don't know what to do from here, I can't say what's wrong or right

Should you keep on fighting
Is now the time to take your rest

I know you'll never give up
I don't know how much fight you have left

The breaths, that you're, now, taking, each, more important than the one before

The time you have left, here on earth, none of us knows, for sure

Let us savor the moments, the moments gone and those that remain

I hope it's true what we've been taught
No matter what, we will see each other again!

POEMS BY KENDALL THOMPSON and VICTORIA THOMPSON

The Pathway

I hear you calling out to our brother
You're seeking help from our mother and dad

I hear you telling them you're ready
You're willing to follow the narrow path

No one can walk there with you
The path is dark and then there's light

Some make their way, in the morning, while others make their way at
night

I hear you calling grandma
I heard a cousin's name or two

First the journey, all by yourself and then, suddenly, there are others with
you

I don't know if they are all listening
I don't know if they are clearing the way

Again, you're saying you're ready
Any help they can give you would be great

When you're ready, throw off all your baggage
There is no need for a hat or a coat

The path is narrow and dimly lit but it is how you come in from the cold!

 POEMS BY KENDALL THOMPSON and VICTORIA THOMPSON

Streetlights

She will walk hand in hand with her maker
She will, in time, find her way

We can wish that she will miraculously heal
We can pray that she could stay

We can hope she has heard our parents, and when the streetlights do
come on

We can hope she tries to beat their glow and hurry herself on home

In time we each must hurry home and heed our parents' advice

I expect you home early tonight, hurry home before the streetlights!

POEMS BY KENDALL THOMPSON and VICTORIA THOMPSON

Paper Thin

He sits there watching, looking for a semblance of what she once was

She lies there being watched wondering if he could imagine the women
with whom he fell in love

He talks to her hoping that she could still understand

She hopes he can see through her anger and knows that she sees an
altruistic man

Were the words last spoken the last between friends

The line between love and hate is paper thin

A weighted heart holds him in place

He sits beside the bedside as she stares off into space

They are tired, and rest is near

Each imagines the future and is gripped by fear

The tears flow from deep within
The moment between life and death is paper thin!

So, his mourning begins!
Even though it is not yet their end!

 POEMS BY KENDALL THOMPSON and VICTORIA THOMPSON

So, I Cry

I sit here and listen as you breathe, and I cry

I think of you and I cry without sound

Words escape me and I cry

I can't write so I cry!

POEMS BY KENDALL THOMPSON and VICTORIA THOMPSON

God's Call

Life is never promised. We live but day to day

When a loved one is taken. We always wish that they could stay

Is it true, death has no number? Is it my time when I am called?

I just feel, my call home early. So let me pray death won't befall

Befall, before my times up. Too soon to end my race

I've only been here a short time. Let this journey remain on pace

I know it seems I am begging. I would surely love more time

My friends I don't want to leave you. I think it's God who is on the line

Would you say, I will; not answer. When it is God who is calling you home

Know I will always be with you. Dare I say you will never be alone

It's my call and I must answer. Our God has made this call

It is my turn to answer. I must leave and I will miss you all!

POEMS BY KENDALL THOMPSON and VICTORIA THOMPSON

Come

Momma, come for your daughter
She is calling out to you

She is ready to make the journey home
There is nothing more we can do

Daddy come get one of your baby girls
She needs to be worry free

Let her come spend more time with you
Let her bounce upon your knee

Brother come gather your sister
Make sure she makes it home

The road just may be a little tough
Make sure she doesn't walk alone

She is calling out to momma
She is calling out to dad

She has called out to our brother
Come to get her and please come fast

The time has come to let her go
Our time to kiss goodbye

The time has come to come get her
We can see it in her eyes!

 POEMS BY KENDALL THOMPSON and VICTORIA THOMPSON

Pierced Silence

Momma was the last word I heard
I heard you scream it twice

A sound that pierced the silence
In the middle of the night

It made me confident
Mom had arrived to take you home

This didn't erase the worry that you still were all alone

I remembered you called for momma
I heard you call her twice

Words I've heard you scream before, in the middle of the night

This time the word screamed differently
This time she had arrived

She came to gently take your hand
She came to be by your side

It seemed to me an exaltation
Momma had finally heard your cry

It was a joyous sound for me
The scream that pierced the silence of that night!

POEMS BY KENDALL THOMPSON and VICTORIA THOMPSON

We Sit, We Wait

We sit impatiently waiting
We sit waiting on a final call

Have you yet to complete your journey
Have you left us once and for all

Has your heart thumped its final beat
Have you breathed your final breath

Have you drifted off to sleep
Have you've started your eternal rest

So we sit and wait impatiently
We wait to know if you've journeyed home

We wait to know if you're still here
We impatiently wait to know if you have gone!

POEMS BY KENDALL THOMPSON and VICTORIA THOMPSON

Prep Work

I am surrounded by the dark of night
The sounds of life are lessening

When will you finally journey home
When will you receive this final blessing

When will there be no more worry
When will a breath be easy to take

When will you receive your wings
It's said God makes no mistakes

In my eyes I see a final struggle
In my heart I am being prepared

You are more than almost home
You are almost there

I can hear your heartbeat quicken
I can see your chest rise decrease

I said my heart was being prepared
I never said that this would be easy!

POEMS BY KENDALL THOMPSON and VICTORIA THOMPSON

Gone On!

You've gone on to meet your maker
You've gone on to claim your prize

You've gone on to take your rest
You've gone on to the other side

Your eyes are no longer open
You can finally rest your eyes

You can sit amongst the roses, while we take a proper cry

You've gone on to bask in glory
You've gone on to give God praise

You've gone on to hug our parents
You've gone on and we are not afraid

You've gone on to prepare a table, where we all will sit one day

You've gone on and we are thankful
You've gone on, in peace, we pray!

POEMS BY KENDALL THOMPSON and VICTORIA THOMPSON

The Expected is Unexpected

We got the call we wanted but did not want
The call we expected but never expected to come

They told us you've taken your final breath
They told us you're now at home

The tears, they fall, from our faces
From our eyes, to our cheeks, to the ground

I will tell you there is nothing normal about today
Our world has been turned upside down

So we've said our final goodbye
We haven't shed our final tears

I will venture to say this is the beginning
We will be still crying in the coming years!

Written by Kendall Thompson
for
Norma Cheryl Thompson Blackmon
02-29-1960
12-03-2019

Can you hear me?

I lay at night and talk aloud, waiting for your reply
I lay in bed and I'm teary eyed, as silence consumes me

If you're always with me, why can't I hear you?

I thought our worlds would collide

I ask you to visit me in my dreams, just to feel you by my side

Patience is certainly a virtue

I'll continue our conversations with faith you'll hear me and I'll hear you
too

By,
Victoria A. Thompson

Tick, Tock

We ignore time, until it begins to run out

When one clock stops, the new clock, of immortality, begins

While you begin a new journey, we rewind our clocks, as we remember,
our time with you

We exit our trances and realize,
time waits for no man, and that life is for the living

The sun will rise and set, a new day will come
We will continue to enjoy life, as long as, our clocks allow

We find solace in knowing your time is now limitless and that, one day,
our clocks will yet again be synchronized

_By,_
Victoria Thompson

POEMS BY KENDALL THOMPSON and VICTORIA THOMPSON

Memories

Our memories together are frozen in time

They are now split in two
Yours up in heaven
And mine here on earth

We will have so much to catch up on,
When the time comes

Or so I think,
you'll probably surprise me,
Telling me all about my happenings
While I eagerly wait to hear yours

At last, our memories together resume

By,
Victoria A. Thompson

Leap Year

Your birthday will happen this year
For many this occurs every year
For you every four

Sixty would be the age
A milestone
But You won't be here to celebrate
As heaven is now your home

Some of us will dial your number
Only to realize you won't pickup
We will shed our tears

Through our tears, we will all speak aloud
to wish you the happiest of birthdays

February 29th
A day we will all speak to you
A day we will all share our fondest memories of and with you

A day that just won't be quite the same

By,
Victoria A. Thompson

POEMS BY KENDALL THOMPSON and VICTORIA THOMPSON

<u>Overcast</u>

Am I selfish for wishing we had more time?

Was twenty-three years' worth of love and memories not enough for me?

*Or maybe when we exchanged our "see you laters" I wasn't ready for
what was yet to come*

Grief!

*You were too sick to live
Yet somehow, I wish you were here*

*I know you're always with me
But my uncertainty of where you are instills fear*

Maybe, just maybe, I need to have a little more faith

We may not have more time together in the same place

But somehow, I know you're near

*By,
Victoria A. Thompson*

One Last Visit

I contemplate visiting your apartment
The most recent one that is

I haven't been since you've passed

I'm not sure if I'm ready to go back
But time is running out
Soon it'll be someone else's humble abode

Those walls hold our final moments together

Though each apartment you inhabited left behind stories for a lifetime,
this apartment is where we shared our final moments of laughter, love,
and sadness

It is only right that I go back one last time

By,
Victoria Thompson

The Closed Backdoor

The sun is out
The breeze is light
The trees cast shade
The Bluetooth speaker is jammin
All that is missing is you

Our season is upon us
Yet you're no longer here
I keep looking at the backdoor,
Waiting to hear "yoohooo" before it opens
It is bittersweet

I look to my left at the chair you'd occupy
The bug spray you'd spray, to mark your territory
It is crazy because I can feel you here
My eyes fill with tears

You're with me no matter my doubts
Your presence today is strong
I'll continue to bask in the sun here on earth as you will in heaven

By,
Victoria A Thompson

One Sided Conversation

I almost called to talk to you
I forgot I could just talk out loud

I could let my voice just carry
Carry toward the distant clouds

There was just one simple problem
One simple problem in all of that

I wouldn't be able to hear your voice
You wouldn't be talking back

So a one sided conversation
I will talk and I hope that you hear

Wait, I thought I heard your voice
Is this my mind playing tricks on my ears?

POEMS BY KENDALL THOMPSON and VICTORIA THOMPSON

In Darkness I Cry

I lay here crying in the dark
Into the heavens, my eyes, set gaze

I am waiting on the light
Then no reason to be afraid

You no longer walk alone
Family again is by your side

I don't know when the light will come
No tears wasted as I lay and cry

On salvation I lay my hopes
Your journey made, now you lay and rest

You have finally made it home
This journey made at "HIS" behest!

POEMS BY KENDALL THOMPSON and VICTORIA THOMPSON

Again I Breathe

It is morning and I have yet to close my eyes
Some continue to question me as to why

I am not afraid!

I cry, uncontrollably, for this new thing, of which, I cannot believe

I blubber out the names of those I don't want to leave

I am a fighter who cannot except defeat

This is the first opponent, that I am sure, to whom, I will not win

Yet I still make my plans!

I will take a walk outside and view the changing in color, of autumn's leaves

I will take in the beauty that is possessed in each and every tree

I feel free!

Now, again I breathe!

POEMS BY KENDALL THOMPSON and VICTORIA THOMPSON

<u>Seasons</u>

I will listen for your heartbeat, in the thunderstorms, in the spring

I will listen, for the sound of your breaths, during hurricane season

I will listen, for your voice, in the snowstorms, in winters to come

I will listen for your footsteps, on the leaves that fall, in autumn

I will look for your earthly shadow, when the sun is, at my back

I will ask, out loud, for your advice, if you can imagine that

I will cry, when it is raining, so others can't see my tears

I will have all of the seasons covered, as I think of you over the years!

Winter, Spring, Summer, and Fall
The seasons bring sudden change

I will simply smile and laugh, at the mention of your name!

POEMS BY KENDALL THOMPSON and VICTORIA THOMPSON

Moments of Sorrow

Our sorrow is just beginning
Our sorrow may never end

There will come another tomorrow and our hearts will begin to mend

We are sorry we've lost our sister, our aunt, his wife, our friend

We are with high expectations, that one day we will see you again

This is only a moment, in a lifetime of moments, that have shaped our lives

Like the moment you took your husband's hand
The moment you became his wife

There were other monumental moments, as when you claimed my daughter as yours

The moments that I read poems to you or the last time you went outdoors

So, you see there will be some sorrow
Sorrow for as long as we might live

In these somber moments, we will simply wipe away our tears!

POEMS BY KENDALL THOMPSON and VICTORIA THOMPSON

<u>Tears Tomorrow</u>

Lots of tears from my eyes today, tomorrow might bring more of the same

It's simply hard to hold back the tears, at the mention of your name

Prepared by yesterday, tomorrow, I have a better plan

I will ready myself to hear your name, in case it's mentioned by chance

How is your sister doing, give her my prayers, tell her I said hello

Condolences to the family, for most people already know

You've finished your earthly journey
You've fought, as is said, the good fight

None of these thoughts can help me, when I lay in bed at night

I hear the Bible verses, the hymnals will be sang

Once again, the tears will flow just as if I am hearing your name!

POEMS BY KENDALL THOMPSON and VICTORIA THOMPSON

Uncontrollable Cry

The tears just seem to flow right now
My heart is overwhelmed

My eyes get full and overflow
This stops then it begins again

Tears that just start flowing
The tears just seem to stream from my eyes

I never seem to know the when
These are, uncontrollable cries

There is a rhyme and reason
You have left for the heavens, above

So, although the cries seem uncontrollable,
it's because I've lost someone I love!

A Sudden Chill

I ran with an open-heart today
I ran under the open sky

I relished in its beauty
I even took a moment, to myself, and cried

I sang, "His Eye is on the Sparrow"
I hummed "Amazing Grace"

I thought about the moment, that again, we would smile, face to face

We will laugh, and make merry our voices
We will plan "our daughter's fate"

We will laugh again and make merry
It's her life, so this would be a mistake

Suddenly I was in the stretch for home
A sudden chill came over me

All thoughts of you, those kept me warm
Near the end of the run, it sure got chilly!

POEMS BY KENDALL THOMPSON and VICTORIA THOMPSON

Just a Whisper

I patiently await a whisper
Have you made it home

Are you still out in the cold
Are you safe and warm

Are our parents with you
Is our brother by your side

Are you just as happy, as you were, when you were alive

Is it your tomorrow
Does time really matter there

I patiently await a whisper
Don't worry, I'm not scared

Well off to sleep I will go
In my dreams, I hope I'll hear

I hope I hear you whisper
Just whisper it in my ear!

POEMS BY KENDALL THOMPSON and VICTORIA THOMPSON

<u>Choked Up!</u>

The cold rain drips, from my brow, as it's headed down my cheeks

My voice is nonexistent, as I am too choked up to speak

My heart is thump, thump, thumping, as if it will beat right through my chest

These are my final thoughts, as we finally lay you down to rest

So again, a see you later but we won't promise not to cry

Look around on every face, you will not see one single dry eye

A Momentary Cry

Today I almost cried for you, ask me what held me back

You would know that I am extremely sad and I thought you wouldn't like that

You see mostly we laughed together, on occasion, we did share a cry

I don't know what else to say, as the tears are falling, from my eyes

I know these people see me crying and wonder what could be the matter

I simply thought of our time with you and the longer I thought about it, it made me sadder

So, I did cry, if only, for a moment
Now again I am wearing a smile

I can't tell you how long the smile will last but
I'm thinking of you and hoping it lasts for a while!

POEMS BY KENDALL THOMPSON and VICTORIA THOMPSON

Pretending

I can't explain to you the disbelief, even though I knew the day would come!

The plan was to make you comfortable; the plan was to see you all the way home

We returned you, to your doorstep, you had to walk in all alone

I don't know how many times I can say it, I cannot believe that you are gone

I can remember the exact moment, when you told me you were ill!

We spoke of beating this opponent, just as if, it was no big deal

I still think you gained your victory, even though you're not here still

You see I now understand, you didn't want to die but you were way too sick to live!

So, I will begin the healing process
I will cry, I will laugh, and then I will cry again

I still won't believe that you have left us
You're still with us is what I will pretend!

Tad Bit Blue

Every song brings a hint of sorrow
Every verse seems a tad bit blue

We are spending our first Christmas, this first one spent, without you

We will still unwrap the presents, we will sing together, Silent Night!

We will raise our glass in toast to you
We will hug each other, especially tight

Ava Maria sung out loudly, in our Latin, of which, we don't know

Little Drummer Boy, off in the distance
Frosty a man of snow

Eighteen Cents, one of your favorites
Hippopotamus is the want for you

The songs of the season sung together
Although there is sorrow and we feel a tad bit blue!

POEMS BY KENDALL THOMPSON and VICTORIA THOMPSON

Purely Day to Day

There is no song you can sing to me, that will take the pain away

There are no magic words or quotes, for me, that you can say

This is purely a time healed sickness
This is purely day to day

The sickness is a broken heart, for my sister is gone away

I know you wish for peace and comfort and for all these things, we will
pray

The healing of this sickness is purely day to day!

This doesn't mean don't sing to me
This doesn't mean I don't want your support

Just continue these things and to pray for me
Day by day they might bring me comfort!

POEMS BY KENDALL THOMPSON and VICTORIA THOMPSON

Heavenly Thoughts

My thoughts today, on the heavens
In the heavens, must be the grandest of times

I am thinking of the people who reside there
In heaven they must be awfully kind

There are mothers and fathers and sisters, grandfathers, grandmothers,
brothers, uncles, and aunts

Just knowing that they are smiling down on me,
gives me reason for heavenly thoughts

My thoughts today are on the heavens
Heavenly thoughts give me reasons to smile

Just thinking of the loved ones who have traveled there

I think I will think of heaven for a little while!

POEMS BY KENDALL THOMPSON and VICTORIA THOMPSON

The Place Where You Lay

I come by purposely to shed a tear
In this, a solemn place

Hoping that the book is true and again we'll be face to face

For now the memories must hold me up, although in time long ago

That you no longer graced this earth
There would be no more hellos

Now we only speak to you in prayers, in dreams, at grave

Where I come to shed a tear
In this place where you'll eternally lay!

POEMS BY KENDALL THOMPSON and VICTORIA THOMPSON

Always Again

You will always be more than just a memory
Your carefree soul has been released

Released to soar in the heavens above
We will, forever, know your love

Love is said to be selflessly blind
We will know your love for the rest of our time

Time for you to take your rest
We question the when, but god knows best

Best, for now, we say, see you later
Death is only a temporary separator

Separator of hugs, not of memories made
I will see you again, so it has been said!

 POEMS BY KENDALL THOMPSON and VICTORIA THOMPSON

Suddenly Peace

You are gone and we will miss you
It is okay for us to cry

You have taken your final journey
We have said to you, goodbye

You have taught us many lessons, through life and now, with death

You will always be here by our sides, but your body must take its rest

One moment, there was a struggle, in the next moment, there was
suddenly peace

You took away our worries, we breathe, a sigh of relief

Our world has lost a hero, the heavens has gained a saint

A simple kiss, laid on your forehead
Poppa, we will see you again!

POEMS BY KENDALL THOMPSON and VICTORIA THOMPSON

Breathe Again

Amongst us, an air of sadness
Our father has gone on to rest

He can speak and sing and laugh again
He is no longer out of breath

He is speaking at the head of the table
He is singing in the all men's choir

He is laughing with his breakfast friends
This he, can now, do for hours

So we've gathered all of our senses
In the air, a sense of joy

The man, who is more than our father
Our poppa can breathe once more!

POEMS BY KENDALL THOMPSON and VICTORIA THOMPSON

Morning Greeting

I wanted to call you to tell you good morning

I did say good morning, but I said it out loud

I screamed it to the heavens, I screamed it towards the clouds

I didn't wait, for confirmation, that you were on the other end

I knew that you would respond right back, if you didn't then I would pretend

I want to call you to tell you good morning

I will just scream it nice and loud

I am guessing this is how we will converse, since your no longer around

I think I will scream out good morning, to you, each and every day

I think I will make this our new daily routine, unless you can tell me there is a better way?

POEMS BY KENDALL THOMPSON and VICTORIA THOMPSON

Life Must Be Lived

Living is not for the faint of heart
It takes courage to live unafraid

Living is not for the faint of heart, for you must live with the mistakes
you've made

Living is not for the faint of heart, you must live life hard day by day

Life is for the living and to live life you must be brave

Live life and live it hard, let your heart know there is no mistake

Live life like there is no tomorrow
Life would not have it any other way!

POEMS BY KENDALL THOMPSON and VICTORIA THOMPSON

Hello

I had a dream during the night
The dream was of you and me, of us

The dream is foggy to my memory
I can't remember much

I do remember you loved me
I do remember your smile

I know it's you just saying hello, in your own quiet and fatherly style

So, I will dream, and I will remember
Some daydreams and others at night

I will dream of us, of you and me
I will dream and all will be alright!

POEMS BY KENDALL THOMPSON and VICTORIA THOMPSON

I Want to Call

I want to call my sister
This is a thought that brings a tear to my eye

I can't tell you why I feel this way
I can't give you a reason why

I want to call my sister
I have a need to hear her voice

I will listen to a tape recording, for this is my only choice

I want to call my sister
So I speak aloud for it's the only way

I will call my sister
I know she hears every word I say

POEMS BY KENDALL THOMPSON and VICTORIA THOMPSON

Broken Heart

I heard that you lost an aunt today
For my uncle, a sister has gone on

I am sure your hearts are heavy
His heart is heavy for his last sister is gone

There are no words of condolence, no words that come to mind

Hold on to the memories, this will help, but it will take time

For now, I shed a tear in thoughts, in thoughts of the family's loss

In time we all must pay a fare
The fare for a loved one is a broken heart!

POEMS BY KENDALL THOMPSON and VICTORIA THOMPSON

Come Home

Come home to me, my servant
You've done all you can do on earth

Travel home, to heaven, where more can know, your worth

Your job as an earthly angel, has come full circle and is now complete

Come home to heaven, your new home, you have earned your heavenly
wings

You've lived a life, heroic, a good father, a husband and friend

You've helped hundreds, without knowing their names, this is the mark of
a good man

Come home to me, my servant, for you have earned your wings

You've done all, on earth, that you can do
It is time for bigger and better things!

POEMS BY KENDALL THOMPSON and VICTORIA THOMPSON

Missing

Missing my aunt's potato salad
Missing my grandmother's sweet tea

Missing my sister's deviled eggs
Missing my mother's roast beef

Missing my father's laughter
Missing my brother's smile

Missing just what you're missing
I've been missing these things for a while

My aunt can make my aunt's potato salad
My cousins, grandma's sweet tea

My daughter can make my sister's deviled eggs
My sisters can make my mom's roast beef

My brother's smile, is in my brothers
My father's laugh can come out of each

Missing doesn't have an ending
Just as good but no replacing!

POEMS BY KENDALL THOMPSON and VICTORIA THOMPSON

__The Lord's Angels__

He surrounds himself with Angels
We question his decisions made

We've asked for more time to spend
Is this not why we have prayed

Did our prayers just go unanswered
Did they fall unto deaf ears

Is this part of learning faith how we must learn to allay our fears

For it's said you're ever present
An omniscient, all knowing being

Is this why each loved one lost
We feel has to get their wings

POEMS BY KENDALL THOMPSON and VICTORIA THOMPSON

All Saints Convention

She is headed towards the convention
This convention attended by saints

Martin, Teresa, Bob Marley
Malcom and Marcus reign

Her train has left the station
for here she no longer resides

She packed her bags for the journey,
Where it is said, again she's alive

Let no friend take worry, let no foe rejoice

The convention is a place where saints, want go,
they want the place by choice

Here she will sit at the table, where her sustenance, prepared
She will sit and convene with the other saints, for she has paid her
earthly fare

Now rejoice that she has made it
Let her sons' and daughters' eyes well

Let them well for she will forever live
You all remain to tell her tale!

POEMS BY KENDALL THOMPSON and VICTORIA THOMPSON

Our First Lesson

I successfully completed my mission
I made it home after my shift

A life of helping others
It has all come down to this

I made it home from the station
The station which was my life

I cherish the friendships that were formed
I cherish my family and my wife

Ring the bell for my service
I've answered my final call

I am now a guardian angel
I will forevermore assist one and all!

POEMS BY KENDALL THOMPSON and VICTORIA THOMPSON

I Will Prevail

Our separation is only temporary
I will again hold you in my arms

You have gone to meet our maker
One day, too, will come along

I wait to hear your chuckle
Your over glasses look

Your falling off to sleep,
as you read your favorite book

This separation is temporary,
you're gone to blaze a trail

We will be reunited, when it's my turn
When it's my turn to prevail!

The Loss of Bubby

Today I felt quite badly, for what I did for me

Of course I felt your anger, I have heartfelt sympathy

Though I came here to support you through this newfound family pain

The fact that I too grieve for him is a fact that still remains

I know he is not my kin folk, but this hurts my heart the same

Just as if my father died a feeling I can't explain

So I'm sorry that the angel, that you gained here through your loss

I will consider an angel gained, but I'll never understand the cost

For now I'll go on praying that he rests a peaceful sleep

This will not control those eyes that feel a must to weep

POEMS BY KENDALL THOMPSON and VICTORIA THOMPSON

The Quiet Whisper

Rest thy gentle Angel
There is nothing left here for you to do

Our Lord has called you home
He must have quietly whispered to you

It truly makes us sad
That he has chosen this, your time to go

We will gently weep for you
For there must be something we do not know

Why did he take a young one
To enter the pearly gates

Why are we left to carry-on
We know not our time or place

For now, we will say our farewells
For you have left your earthly home

Now you reside in heaven
In God's place you'll forever roam!

<u>Rest In Peace</u>

I don't need to know what you died of I, just simply, need to know that you've died

Knowing that you are no longer with us, is reason enough for me to cry

I don't need one's confirmation that you were lovable or you were the best

I need to know that you are safely home and, in God's house, you will eternally rest

Rest In Peace young Angel, your earthly chores are complete

Now the only thing left to do, I have said it before, is for you to Rest In Peace!

POEMS BY KENDALL THOMPSON and VICTORIA THOMPSON

My Way

When it is your time to go
Will you be the one who knows?

Will you hold on too long?
Will you hold on too long
when your body is no longer strong?

Will you gracefully bow out?
Will you leave, with still a doubt?

Is this decision made, a dud or is it great?

Well, I'll tip my hat and to black I'll fade
I will always know, I did this "my way"

 POEMS BY KENDALL THOMPSON and VICTORIA THOMPSON

The Grand Miracle

Death is never pretty
For in the end it is still death

It will often leave you wondering
What is it that I have left

Death should be thought of in this way
A punctuation to a grand miracle

For now the miracle known as life
The miracle has come full circle

POEMS BY KENDALL THOMPSON and VICTORIA THOMPSON

Our Brother's Son

Our brother lost a son today
The neighborhood lost a lad

Our brother's son has gone away
His departure has made us sad

We weep for our brother's sorrow
Our eyes well, for he has lost

We hold him in our heart's space
We will keep him in our thoughts

Our sorrows for your loss of son
We can't tell you how to grieve

Let us hold you in our arms, my friend
Let us, too, all bereaved

 POEMS BY KENDALL THOMPSON and VICTORIA THOMPSON

Rest Easy

Oh, woe is me, woe is me
What am I to do

We have been together for such a long, long time
Who do I now have to turn to?

Who will wipe my brow, of sweat?
when the temperature is extremely high

Who will help me wish upon a star,
as it shoots across the sky

I know I will feel your spirit
Your presence I will never know

I am happy that I will know you're there,
no matter where I go

So, my spirit will rest easy,
now I need yours
to rest easy as well

My hopes that we will meet again,
but only time will tell

POEMS BY KENDALL THOMPSON and VICTORIA THOMPSON

Rest My Brother

Rest my weary servant,
you've languished far too long

You will now know the perfect place,
that you've heard about in song

The place, where rests your mother,
the place where your sister resides

The place, where you enter through the pearly gates,
where it's said again your alive

You've left your earthly body,
Your spirit has been set free

Rest thy weary servant,
Would you save a place for me?

 POEMS BY KENDALL THOMPSON and VICTORIA THOMPSON

Rest My Weary

How the time has passed us by
I don't know where to begin

You are not just a sister
You are one of our best friends

You've sacrificed your freedoms
So we could tag along

You took the blame for our mistakes
You strengthened the family bond

You mother, when need be,
You made certain we did little crime

Now you give the lesson
None of us can stop the time

So rest my weary sister
Did I say you are a dear friend

Forever know you are on our minds
Our hearts will forever be on the mend!

POEMS BY KENDALL THOMPSON and VICTORIA THOMPSON

Resting Place

I look back for you're a memory
I can no longer see you face to face

I think back and my remembrances
Each one brings a smile to my face

I have pictures that give me image
I can still hear your voice in my ears

Each time one of you left us
Each time our eyes couldn't hold the tears

I wave and say a gentle hello
I still pass and never cease to wave

I am reminded that life is to be lived
In order to live you mustn't be afraid

POEMS BY KENDALL THOMPSON and VICTORIA THOMPSON

<u>*Somber Moments*</u>

The crush and devastation that comes with sad news

I am sure that this is painful and my hearts, it aches for you

This unbelievable moment that no parent should have to face

The loss of one of their children, for they can never be replaced

There are no words of comfort, from me to you, that I can share

I have never experienced such sorrow, so I do not dare compare

Another's somber moment, that in their lives they faced

I hope that all of your memories, will keep in your heart's space

So take with you well wishes, at this moment that is so low

Know you know a sorrow that not all of us will know

I wish that I can help you but I am just a man

So, I hope you find the comfort that he is now in God's hands!

POEMS BY KENDALL THOMPSON and VICTORIA THOMPSON

Dearly Departed

The joy of life is living, even though we know we'll die
Isn't there a chance at living, known as the after life

Your faith which has shaped your future
You'll see them all again

Your mother, father, your brother
Your wife, your sister, and friends

The streets are lined with gold
The colors will blend as one

The place we know as heaven
Where God sits with his son

So fret you not of dying
Fret not for those who dearly depart

For death is not the end of their life
For the believer it is just the start!

 POEMS BY KENDALL THOMPSON and VICTORIA THOMPSON

The Lady Sleeps

I speak now, of the death, of a lady
She now rests in eternal sleep

I think of the son and daughter she borne
For the family she leaves, I now weep

I speak, of the death, of a lady
My eyes well, for she has left them alone

In her faith. she's headed to the mountain top

She's headed to the place, Christians call home

So I speak, of the rebirth, of a lady

She now lives forever in Christ

The rebirth of the lady is evident

She now joins her parents and brother, in life after life!

Never Ending Journey

Our never-ending journey,
the journey that starts at birth
and begins again at death

This journey filled with amazing things
and begins again
when there are only memories left

From the time that you first cry,
you crawl, and then you take your first step

The journey is more like an endurance race,
at the end of it, there will be time to rest

The never-ending journey begins at birth and the memories
keep you alive after death

POEMS BY KENDALL THOMPSON and VICTORIA THOMPSON

Whispers

I can hear the whispers of my forefathers
The voices are carried by the winds

I hear whispers of my mother's moms
I hear whispers of long-lost friends

I hear whispers in the daytime
I hear whispers in the night

I hear whispers for me to come on home and head into the heavenly light

I hear whispers, I hear voices, I hear songs, of strength and faith

I hear whispers of my maker, who I will soon meet face to face

I hear whispers and to the whisperers, I sometimes whisper back

I will see you when I am ready, and it won't be a moment before that!

POEMS BY KENDALL THOMPSON and VICTORIA THOMPSON

ACKNOWLEDGEMENTS

It is not easy when we lose those that we love. We will all have to travel that lonely road. Thank you to everyone who reads these messages from our hearts. Although this is dedicated to our loved ones, there are poems that have been written for you. Thank you all for reading our poems!

ABOUT THE AUTHOR

Kendall Thompson dedicated his life to protecting his community as a Firefighter. He's a member of a proud African American family with deep roots in Alexandria Virginia and a history of community service. Kendall is a long-distance runner and family man. His poems spring from his soul as he struggles to balance his lifetime of service with his lifetime of racial disregard. His poetry is his quiet call to action, expressing his belief in the power of shared understanding.

"I HEAR WHISPERS" is the author's third book of verse. He has also written WHY WE WALK IN THE STREET and Angry Black Man.

Made in the USA
Columbia, SC
15 January 2025

51865084R00067